UN AMBASSADOR

A Behind-the-Scenes Look at Madeleine Albright's World

ROBERT MAASS

WALKER AND COMPANY NEW YORK

Dedicated to the memory of my father,
Ernest Maass, who worked for and cared deeply
about the United Nations.

First published in the United States of America in 1995 by Walker Publishing Company, Inc.
Published simultaneously in Canada by Thomas Allen & Son Canada, Limited,
Markham, Ontario

Library of Congress Cataloging-in-Publication Data
Maass, Robert.
UN Ambassador : a behind-the-scenes look at Madeleine Albright's world / Robert Maass.
p. cm.
ISBN 0-8027-8355-4 (hc). — ISBN 0-8027-8356-2 (reinforced)
1. Albright, Madeleine Korbel—Juvenile literature. 2. Albright, Madeleine Korbel—Pictorial
works—Juvenile literature. 3. United Nations—Officials and employees—Biography—Juvenile
literature. 4. Ambassadors—United States—Biography—Juvenile literature. I. Title
E840.8.A37M33 1995
327.73'0092-dc20 [B] 95-14660
CIP AC

Unless otherwise noted, photographs are © Robert Maass.

Book design by Diane Stevenson of Snap-Haus Graphics

Printed in Hong Kong

2 4 6 8 10 9 7 5 3 1

★

Walker and Company wishes to thank Ambassador Albright and her staff for all their time
and assistance with this project.

Madeleine in London in 1945. (ALBRIGHT FAMILY PHOTOGRAPH)

America's ambassador to the United Nations, Madeleine Albright, had the perfect childhood for a diplomat. By the time she was eleven, Madeleine had lived in five different countries. As a small girl, she left her native country of Czechoslovakia and became a refugee of the Second World War raging in Europe. Her father was a diplomat who was part of the Czechoslovak government in exile in London, and Madeleine lived through the bombing raids there, called the blitz. "I spent a lot of time during the war in air-raid shelters or playing under a big steel table we had, so that if the house collapsed during a bombing I'd be all right." Her wartime experiences made Madeleine grow up quickly.

Madeleine (far left) in a traditional Czechoslovak costume, with her family. (ALBRIGHT FAMILY PHOTOGRAPH)

Madeleine Albright didn't go to school to become a diplomat, but she did get an early start. "I grew up as the child of a diplomat," she says. "My father was a strong influence on my life and what I have become. We talked about international relations all the time—the way some families talk about sports or other things around the dinner table." Wearing traditional Czechoslovak dress, young Madeleine would sometimes greet visiting dignitaries when her father was the Czechoslovak ambassador to Yugoslavia. "The little girl at the airport who used to greet important visitors—that was me. I used to do it for a living." Little could she have imagined then that she would later return to her native land as the United States ambassador to the United Nations, accompanying the president of the United States.

When the war was over, Madeleine was sent to a school in Switzerland where she had to learn to speak French. It was the fourth language she learned, and she was just ten years old! Madeleine grew up understanding that she had to get along and adapt to new situations. That quality would always serve her well. "As a child, living in so many foreign countries made it easier for me to adjust to different situations and to make friends. My mother always taught me to be open and friendly with new people. She said I could learn a lot from them, and she was right."

More than forty years after Madeleine's family fled the Communist regime there, democracy finally returned to Czechoslovakia in 1989.

In 1948 Madeleine's parents decided to move secretly to the United States, because a Communist government had taken over Czechoslovakia. They did not want to live under an undemocratic system. It was difficult to leave, Madeleine remembers. "My mother had to pretend she was taking our family from Czechoslovakia on a week's vacation, when we were really leaving for good."

They arrived in America with only their suitcases in their hands. The rest of their belongings were left far behind in Europe. As a refugee during the war, Madeleine had seen the U.S. Army arrive to save Europe. The United States became a symbol to the young girl of what was good and just. When her family arrived here with next to nothing, people proved her faith in her new country was well placed. Many new friends helped her family to get a fresh start.

Madeleine's family decided to settle in Denver, where her father began teaching at a university and her mother worked in the public schools. Madeleine loved her new home, but her refugee experience left her with a strong interest in world affairs. "Wherever I went to school, I started an International Relations Club, and because I started it I'd become its president. I'm sure some of my friends found me very boring, but that was what I was interested in, so that's what I did."

After graduating from Wellesley College, Madeleine married and had a family of three girls. During this period she continued to study and work toward her doctorate in political science. Sometimes she thought her studies would never end, but she was determined to complete them, not just for herself but as an example to her daughters. If she could stick to it and finish, no matter how long it took, she would be showing her children that anything can be accomplished with hard work and determination. Madeleine believes that "whatever job you have to do, do it well, because people remember. Even if you're

Madeleine and friends at Wellesley College in Massachusetts. (Madeleine is on the right.) (ALBRIGHT FAMILY PHOTOGRAPH)

Madeleine's 1955 high school portrait. (ALBRIGHT FAMILY PHOTOGRAPH)

not making foreign policy, people remember the job you did."

After completing her university studies, Madeleine Albright worked for many years as an adviser on international affairs to some of the country's most important politicians. All her hard work brought her to the attention of the most important politician in the country. Days after his election, President Clinton's staff called Madeleine to see if she would be interested in a job as the U.S. Ambassador to the United Nations. If so, could she fly down to Arkansas immediately? "It was a little sticky, because I was hosting a party the next evening, and they told me not to tell anyone where I was going."

After a long meeting with the president-elect, Madeleine was asked to take the job. She immediately accepted. Her three children were brought to Arkansas and were proudly by her side the following day, when the president told the world that Madeleine Albright was his choice to represent America at the United Nations.

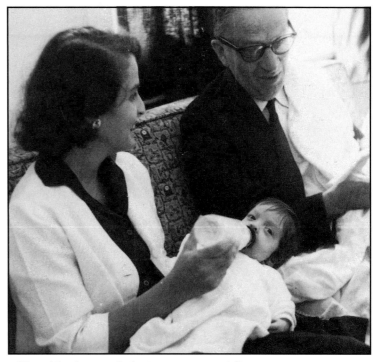

Madeleine with her father and her daughter Alice in October 1961.
(ALBRIGHT FAMILY PHOTOGRAPH)

President-elect Clinton announces Madeleine Albright, the new UN Ambassador. (AP/WIDE WORLD PHOTOS)

Ambassador Albright is proud that the president appointed a woman to head the United States delegation. The world of diplomacy has traditionally been dominated by men. Of the 185 countries at the United Nations, only five delegations—the United States, Jamaica, Kazakhstan, Liechtenstein, and Trinidad and Tobago—are headed by women. Madeleine believes women are particularly well suited for her kind of work. They are expected to handle many different roles at the same time. Working, raising children, and keeping their homes running smoothly is excellent training for the demands of a job where many issues must be juggled at once. Ambassador Albright has worked actively to advance opportunities for women in the foreign service and in national affairs.

The UN organization and its role in world affairs has expanded dramatically since it was founded in 1945. The

United Nations promotes peace among nations and works to improve the standard of living for all the people of the earth. When a war breaks out, like the war in the former Yugoslavia, the United Nations steps in to try to get the two sides to agree to peace. When refugees stream out of a country because of war or famine, as in Rwanda or Somalia, the United Nations organizes relief efforts to bring food, medicine, and shelter to the homeless refugees. When the nations of the world decide that rules must be made to protect the environment, they negotiate and sign treaties under the umbrella of the United Nations, as they did at the Rio summit in 1992.

Ambassador Albright speaks with student interns who spend the summer working at the United Nations.

The United Nations is the center stage of world diplomacy. As the United States ambassador to the United Nations, Madeleine Albright plays a major role in shaping the policies of the world body.

The United Nations was created after the long and bloody Second World War. Ambassador Albright explains, "Today people are used to the fact that there were two world wars, but after the Second World War there was this disbelief that so many people could have died about something that could have been avoided." The original members wanted to form an international organization that would use the art of negotiation to prevent future wars. Since its founding, membership has more than tripled, representing nearly every nation of the world.

Facing page: Each morning, UN guards raise the 185 flags of the member nations of the organization.

Ambassador Albright addressing the Security Council about the Haiti crisis.

President
Clinton,
speaking to the
opening session
of the UN
General
Assembly in
October 1993.

"The General Assembly is a huge room where every country not only is represented but has an equal vote. A little island nation has the same vote as, say, France. It's taught me an incredible respect for each country's individuality and importance. It's like a puzzle, where every piece is important. And, like a puzzle, if pieces are missing it is ruined. What's difficult today is that the puzzle has been broken down to even smaller pieces, which makes it slow and hard to put together."

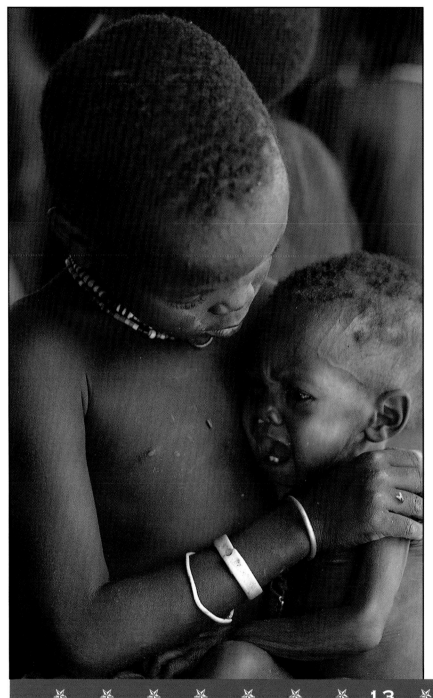

Why is the United Nations so important? It's a place where the whole world is represented and nations can talk to one another to work out differences. "The UN is best at trying to work out a world in which we're all going to live in the future, where there's no starvation, wars, diseases, or refugees. The UN is very important for the children of the world, both to help them now and to ensure that the world is in better shape when they become adults. It's the only organization that can worry about all our international needs, like global warming or refugees or AIDS. The UN can make a dent.

Children at a feeding center in Juba, Sudan. They are refugees from a civil war being fought there.

"The UN is a world in microcosm. In the space of an hour you can see people of all different races, colors, and religions—working together. You get the feeling that the whole world is there in the room—and they set out their arguments in a very calm way, and you realize that it's possible for people to talk things through. It's also fascinating that people talk in so many different languages, which are all being translated as they speak. So even though we're being spoken to in a different language, we can understand and do something together. You start to feel that we all have the same things in common."

UN delegates seated behind Ambassador Albright wear special headphones so speeches can be heard immediately in each one's native language.

Think of the world without a United Nations. Diseases like smallpox, once the killer of millions, have been wiped out thanks to UN efforts. When people become refugees, only the United Nations is able to bring the resources together to help. Many starving people wouldn't survive without relief from UN agencies. The United Nations has also started more than twenty-five peacekeeping operations since its founding. So the United Nations has a vital role to play. "All of us are affected by problems around the world. Many refugees come to the United States and will end up in communities across the country. But if you have an organization that promotes people talking to each other to work out conflicts, they may be able to live peacefully and in good health in the country where they were born."

American grain arrives in Sudan.

A reading class in an elementary school in Phai Sali District, Thailand.

It takes a lot of people to keep the United Nations running smoothly. Just the United States Mission to the United Nations alone, led by Ambassador Albright, includes a staff of more than 100 people. Madeleine must work with her staff to make sure that American interests are served in any resolutions, agreements, or treaties negotiated at the United Nations. At the Friday morning staff meeting, the ambassador briefs her staff and is updated by them on the most important and timely issues of the week.

Ambassador Albright is briefed by an aide on her way from her office in the mission.

The ambassador runs through her day at a fast pace. As she dashes from her office for a Security Council consultation, an aide grabs her for a last-minute meeting. "Here are the key points we believe will be brought up by the nonaligned nations at today's consultation," he advises. En route to the Secretariat building, where the Security Council meets, her press secretary warns her that members of the media are waiting to ambush her with questions. Crossing First Avenue to the UN compound, they review what questions may come up and how they can best be answered.

Even walking across the street to the Secretariat building is an opportunity for aides to meet with the ambassador.

Fielding questions from the press is an important part of Ambassador Albright's job.

As they enter the building, a reporter yells out, "Will the United States call for military intervention in Haiti, Madame Ambassador?" Ambassador Albright is often called upon to explain U.S. foreign policy decisions. She answers a few questions before heading into the meeting.

"Last question, we're late for the meeting," her press secretary says as she recaps the major points to the reporters. They are looking for headline news. "But, Ambassador, how will the United States react—" yells a journalist, but the Ambassador must leave for her meeting.

Official meetings are important, but many top-level conversations take place in busy hallways. After a long

consultation, an African delegate catches Ambassador Albright on her way back to the mission. "Madame Ambassador, may I have your attention for a moment? My government needs some clarification on the United States' position presented today."

Later that afternoon, Guntis Ulmanis, president of the newly independent country of Latvia, stops by to pay a visit. Ambassador Albright usually meets with the most important visiting dignitaries who come to the United Nations. This is a way for her to establish a personal connection with world leaders and to learn firsthand of their priorities and goals.

Ambassador Albright meets Guntis Ulmanis, the president of the recently independent state of Latvia, at the mission. Many foreign leaders meet privately with Ambassador Albright when they come to the United Nations.

Passing through the UN halls, Ambassador Albright stops for an informal meeting with a colleague from one of the Arab States.

As head of the mission, Ambassador Albright tries to get to know all her staff, from top to bottom, by hosting periodic lunches at her official residence in the Waldorf-Astoria Towers. It is a large and elegant suite of rooms with dramatic views of the city. This has been the UN ambassador's official residence for over thirty years. It is a place not only to live but also to entertain important guests.

At a breakfast in her official residence in the Waldorf-Astoria Towers, Ambassador Albright introduces President Clinton's Special Adviser for Haiti, William Gray, to officials.

Ambassador Albright hosts one of her periodic lunches for the mission staff at the residence.

The ambassador may host one or more lunches or dinners a week. Diplomats are expected to entertain as part of their job. It is no secret that important decisions are sometimes made over a relaxing dinner.

At an evening dinner at the residence, Ambassador Albright chats with guest of honor, singer Barbra Streisand.

The entrance to the ambassador's official residence, on the top floor of the Waldorf-Astoria Towers.

Although New York is her base, a typical day for Ambassador Albright can just as easily unfold in Washington, D.C., where she participates in many high-level meetings.

Ambassador Albright leaves her residence at the Waldorf as the city is beginning to come alive. A waiting limousine whisks her to the 7:00 A.M. shuttle, a New York–Washington commuter flight, which she takes so often that the airline staff all know her. "Good morning,

Ambassador Albright boards a shuttle flight to Washington, D.C.

Ambassador," the copilot says as she is seated. She'll use this time—it is a short, fifty-minute flight—to browse the morning papers and maybe catch a few more minutes of sleep.

Ambassador Albright takes a quick catnap on the shuttle flight. Working very long hours, the ambassador tries to rest a little wherever she can.

Ambassador
Albright is on the
phone as soon as
she arrives in
Washington and
consults with her
staff on her way
from the airport
to the State
Department.

The ambassador grabs the car phone as soon as she is picked up for the short drive from the airport to her office at the State Department. The State Department is the headquarters of all United States foreign policy. It is run by the secretary of state, America's chief official for foreign policy.

"Good morning , Elaine. How're we set up for the next few hours?" Elaine Shocas is the ambassador's chief of staff and advises Madeleine on her meetings in D.C. Although the ambassador will see Elaine in a few minutes at her office, her day is so busy that every moment counts.

The State Department headquarters, Washington, D.C.

Left:
Ambassador
Albright walking
down the hall of
the sixth floor of
the State
Department,
where high
officials of the
department have
their offices.

Elaine greets her at the door with a stack of files. "Here are some new documents to review before the 11:00 A.M. NSC [National Security Council] meeting," she says. The ambassador has only a few minutes at her desk before the first of many meetings that day. She meets with the secretary of state, Warren Christopher, as well as several key deputies. Today the country of Haiti is high on the agenda of topics, as refugees have been streaming into south Florida to escape the oppressive conditions of their home. "We are close to agreement for a Security Council resolution on the economic sanctions against Haiti," she tells Secretary Christopher.

Facing page:
Ambassador
Albright consults
with Secretary of
State Warren
Christopher,
America's head of
foreign policy.

Ambassador Albright again makes use of the car phone on her way to the White House.

Within the hour the ambassador is back in her car and on the way to the White House. Madeleine admits, "I do have a bit of 'telephone-itis.'" Even on a ten-block drive, she calls Elaine again from the car. Kevin, the ambassador's security agent, uses his walkie-talkie to call ahead to alert the White House gate that the ambassador's car will be pulling up in sixty seconds.

At the White House, Ambassador Albright attends a meeting of the Principals Committee of the National Security Council. The NSC pulls together the views of different government agencies whose responsibility is national security. The Principals Committee is attended by cabinet-level officials. The cabinet is made up of the people the president chose to run the key government departments. Today's meeting includes Ambassador Albright, the secretaries of state and defense, the attorney general (the Justice Department), the director of the Central Intelligence Agency (CIA), and the chairman of the Joint Chiefs of Staff (the most senior officer of all the armed forces), and it is chaired by the national security adviser. Such meetings are called when important policy decisions need to be made and the views of the different agencies are required. For example, if the United States is dealing with a large number of refugees trying to enter the country, as happened with a sudden stream of Haitian boat people, there are many problems that U.S. leaders must resolve. The Principals Committee would take up such an issue. They often meet two or three times a week.

Ambassador Albright arrives at the White House for a meeting of the National Security Council.

After the meeting, Ambassador Albright speaks with General Shalikashvili, chairman of the Joint Chiefs of Staff, about the navy's role in picking up the refugees fleeing on rickety, unseaworthy boats.

"Our ships are having a hard time housing the numbers of people on those boats. Some of the refugee vessels are capsizing. We're looking at some nearby islands as possible temporary processing centers for these people. Are any governments in the region willing to assist us?" the general asks.

"We've begun discussions with some of the Caribbean governments," the ambassador replies. "I'll be looking into this later today and tomorrow at the UN with their ambassadors. I'll get back to you tomorrow afternoon."

Back at her State Department office, Madeleine barely has a moment to eat a bite of lunch before her schedule calls for another meeting. She meets President Clinton's Special Adviser for Haiti, William Gray, who is trying to negotiate with the Haitian government for a peaceful and humane resolution of the problems there.

The ambassador has to eat a quick lunch at her desk before setting off for her next scheduled meeting.

Ambassador Albright meets with William Gray and military officials to examine alternatives for dealing with refugees fleeing Haiti.

Military officials brief Ambassador Albright on possible sites to house Haitian refugees.

"We've still got a ways to go," Gray says. "The Haitian president has some concerns about the upcoming Security Council vote on sanctions. If we change some of the resolution's language, I think we'll gain his full support."

"I think we can work that out," Ambassador Albright replies. "I'd like you to speak with the Haitians here about the refugees. We're considering some of the nearby islands for temporary housing of these people."

After another late-afternoon NSC meeting at the White House, the ambassador is driven back to the airport for the 7:00 P.M. flight to New York. It's been a long and busy day, but those who guide the nation's foreign relations can't keep to a nine-to-five schedule.

By participating in the cabinet and on the Principals Committee, Ambassador Albright helps shape American foreign policy. Being briefed at the highest levels also means that she is seen by other ambassadors as the president's personal representative to the United Nations. Other governments also know that, when they talk to her, their concerns will be heard at the highest levels of the United States government. "Today I'm in Washington, and when I get back to New York I'll be able to tell them a little more about what our thinking is on a particular issue. And the other way around, I give D.C. real-time knowledge of what's happening at the UN. I see more foreigners per day than anyone else in the administration. I'm on the front lines of foreign policy every day, interpreting how people are relating to our foreign policy."

Ambassador Albright in her office at the State Department.

Ambassador Albright explains U.S. policy to interviewer Bryant Gumbel, host of the morning news program *Today*.

After a full day in Washington, Madeleine Albright will again rise with the sun, to appear as a guest on the early-morning television show *Today*. As the world follows the plight of the Haitian boat people, the American media want the inside track on what the president is thinking. They ask the ambassador to explain the latest developments. One of Ambassador Albright's most important roles is as a senior spokesperson for American foreign policy. "I have been asked to take on a large media role, and I think it makes a big difference," she says. "It's the way the American people get information." Whether she holds a press conference, grants a private interview, or talks to the public via television news shows, she is explaining the country's position. "We are in a period of foreign policy when all the rules are different. It's not easy to explain, because the media often do not allow you to have long conversations. But it's important to use whatever time one has to talk to the public, because in a democracy you have to have public support for policy."

After a speech in Boston, Ambassador Albright is interviewed by some local reporters. She is constantly communicating with the media.

Ambassador Albright has remarked that the TV news networks, like CNN, are really "the sixteenth member of the Security Council." They spread news of policy developments, which generates a reaction almost immediately in capitals around the world. Anything Madeleine Albright may say to the press will be understood as the official position of the United States. She must therefore be careful when commenting on matters that will affect sensitive areas of foreign policy.

The media often want short, simple answers to questions that require longer, more complicated explanations. Ambassador Albright is considered among the most skilled of the administration's foreign policy team for dealing with media interviews. "People tell me I come across well on television because I state things clearly. Perhaps that comes from my years of being a teacher."

Ambassador Albright is greeted by graduate students at Harvard University's Kennedy School of Government. She uses her speech to clarify U.S. foreign policy.

At a speech in Boston, Ambassador Albright fields a question from a member of the audience.

In addition to her media appearances, Ambassador Albright is in demand as a speaker to a wide range of groups, from college graduates to members of public policy associations. The ambassador uses her speeches and media appearances to explain American foreign policy and to build understanding for it. For example, in Boston, she addresses professionals and future public officials whose support is needed to carry out the president's foreign policy.

Facing page: Ambassador Albright working in her office at the U.S. Mission to the UN, directly across the street from the United Nations.

Ambassador
Albright voting
in the UN
Security Council.

Madeleine Albright is a living example of the American Dream. After arriving in America as a refugee, she worked hard and reached the peak of recognition and responsibility in her chosen field. She believes her success is an enormous tribute to the ideals and rights granted to American citizens.

"I get a big kick sitting behind the sign at the UN that says 'United States.' I think it's stunning. The United States has been so incredibly generous to my family that I feel it is the right thing to do whatever I can for American interests at the UN, and to make the United Nations more useful to the world."

What Is the
United Nations?

The United Nations is made up of six main branches—the Security Council, the General Assembly, the Economic and Social Council, the Trusteeship Council, the International Court of Justice, and the Secretariat. Alongside these main branches there are seventeen other intergovernmental "special agencies" that function within the UN. One of the most well-known agencies, UNICEF, is for children. Its letters originally stood for United Nations International Children's Emergency Fund (now it is known as United Nations Children's Fund). Although all the organizations have particular names, they all are considered parts of what is known as simply the United Nations.

The Security Council

The Security Council is the main peacemaking and peacekeeping body of the United Nations. Members suggest courses of action by proposing resolutions—or official agreements—which all the council members vote on. At least nine members of the fifteen-nation council have to vote yes on any resolution to pass it. If one of the five permanent members—the United States, the Russian Federation, France, Britain, and China—votes against the resolution, called a veto, it cannot pass. The council's decisions must be enforced according to the UN Charter. The resolutions passed cover many areas. To help end the fighting in Somalia and bring food to its starving people, the United Nations began a major mission by sending in a large peacekeeping force. To set the stage for a free and democratic election in Cambodia, the United Nations voted to provide peacekeepers made up of soldiers from many countries to monitor the voting. Following the Gulf War, the United Nations voted to impose a trade embargo with Iraq, preventing all countries represented by the United Nations from trading with that government.

One of the most important tasks of the Security Council is nominating the secretary general. He is the United Nations' chief operating officer and its most visible spokesperson. The council meets whenever necessary and in recent years has become the most important world body to work out conflicts between nations. The United States, as a permanent member with veto power, plays a crucial role on the council.

Ambassador Albright with the secretary general of the United Nations, Boutros-Boutros Ghali, in his office.

Members of the Security Council can meet privately in small consultation rooms.

The General Assembly

The General Assembly is where many major decisions are made. Each of the 185 member countries represented, no matter how big or small, has one vote. The most important of the organization's issues, like security or peacekeeping or the budget, are debated in the assembly. Matters of utmost importance require two thirds of the countries to vote yes in order to pass a resolution. Other votes need a simple majority. The General Assembly considers many issues, although most pressing matters of security and peace are taken up by the smaller Security Council. The representatives gather from mid-September through December each year.

The opening session of each year's General Assembly draws many heads of state, foreign ministers, and important dignitaries. They come to New York to present their views of the most significant issues facing the organization and what actions should be taken up by the United Nations. Much of the work carried out by the staff of the organization is determined by the debates and proposals that come out of the General Assembly.

Nelson Mandela of
South Africa
addresses the
General Assembly.

✳ ✳ ✳ ✳ United Nations Annual Observances ✳ ✳ ✳ ✳

March 2—International Women's Day

March 21—International Day for the Elimination of Racial Discrimination

June 4—International Day of Innocent Children Victims of Aggression

Third Tuesday in September—International Day of Peace

First Monday in October—Universal Children's Day

October 1—International Day for the Elderly

October 16—World Food Day

October 24—United Nations Day

December 1—World AIDS Day

December 10—Human Rights Day

✳ ✳ ✳ ✳ To Learn More About the United Nations ✳ ✳ ✳ ✳

Brenner, Barbara. *The United Nations Fiftieth Anniversary Book.* New York: Macmillan, 1995.

Gikow, Louise, and Ellen Weiss. *For Every Child a Better World.* New York: Western, 1993.

Greene, Carol. *The United Nations.* Chicago: Children's Press, 1983.

Jacobs, William J. *Search for Peace: The Story of the United Nations.* New York: Scribner's, 1994.

Pollard, Michael. *United Nations.* New York: Macmillan, 1994.

Stein, R. Conrad. *The Story of the United Nations.* Chicago: Children's Press, 1986.